Amish Prayers

A COLORING BOOK

 **Herald Press**

Harrisonburg, Virginia

The prayers in this coloring book are excerpted and adapted with permission from *Prayer Book for Earnest Christians* (Die ernsthafte Christenpflicht), translated and edited by Leonard Gross (Scottdale, PA: Herald Press, 1997). All rights reserved.

All Scripture quotations, unless otherwise indicated, are taken from the Holy Bible, New International Version®, NIV®. Copyright ©1973, 1978, 1984, 2011 by Biblica, Inc.™ Used by permission of Zondervan. All rights reserved worldwide. www.zondervan.com The "NIV" and "New International Version" are trademarks registered in the United States Patent and Trademark Office by Biblica, Inc.™

AMISH PRAYERS
© 2017 by Herald Press, Harrisonburg, Virginia 22802
    All rights reserved.
International Standard Book Number: 978-1-5138-0156-8
Printed in Canada
Illustrations by Lynn Sommer (www.lynnsommer.com)
Design by Merrill Miller

For orders or information, call 800-245-7894 or visit HeraldPress.com.

21 20 19 18 17   10 9 8 7 6 5 4 3 2 1

Notes on *Amish Prayers from an Amish Mother*

Having grown up in an Amish home in Bird-in-Hand, Pennsylvania, I have a cherished childhood memory of kneeling beside my father while he prayed the evening prayer from *Die ernsthafte Christenpflicht* (*Prayer Book for Earnest Christians*). The prayers in this coloring book are excerpted from this centuries-old prayer book. They are paired with fraktur, a Pennsylvania Dutch folk art developed in the eighteenth and nineteenth centuries that features calligraphy text and ornamental designs drawn from daily life.

I cannot describe the depth of the peace that would overtake my childish heart and mind as my father would pray. Now that I am married, we still use this prayer book with our own children, endeavoring to pass on this same legacy to the next generation.

These prayers are meaningful to me because they were written by our Anabaptist forebears hundreds of years ago while they were encountering severe persecution. I feel this enhances their meaning. It's amazing that they have stood the test of time and are still in use today.

Why do we pray? It's because we are a sinful, fallen human race and we need our Savior's help to live a victorious life, no matter what we're facing. We want to be sheltered from danger, we need God's blessings on our work, our ministers need to be faithful shepherds and teachers, and we want our government not to abuse its power.

Our enemies need prayer too, and as we pray for them, we'll find peace for ourselves.

I believe that prayers from our own hearts are important. The beauty of these humble, unselfish, and heartfelt prayers, however, are unlike anything I could come up with on my own. Like Bible passages, they are always nice and refreshing if I shut out earthly things and let the words guide my thoughts.

In the morning, the prayers for the beginning of a new day fill our souls with fresh hope as we ponder their meaning. There is no earthly care that cannot be brought to the throne of grace. The prayers give me fresh hope, help me anchor myself in God's love and grace, and remind me that heaven is our goal and that our lives here, with their earthly cares and trials, are only temporary. The prayers help us remember the sick and suffering, our government, and our schools, as well as our ministers and widows and orphans.

These prayers remind us of our utter dependence on and need for God and his help in all things. Repentance and confession are a constant theme, with a plea for the Holy Spirit. These prayers ask for God's protection and blessing, intercede for the body of Christ as a whole all over the world, and acknowledge how God sees and knows all our hearts and minds, thoughts and plans. He knows all secrets, so we ask him to give us wisdom so we may earnestly fear him.

That we may lead a quiet and peaceful life in all godliness, peace, and unity is our prayer. This is our prayer for our community and for each home as well. These gifts are divine and cannot be attained by human effort. Only God can give them, and as we humble ourselves and pray and seek God above all else, may he hear from heaven and heal our land. If we pray, all our brokenness and earthly trials will work for our good and for the good of those around us.

May these prayers draw you nearer to God, and may his presence be more real to you than ever before.

The writer belongs to the Old Order Amish and wishes to remain unnamed. She lives with her husband and seven children on a dairy farm in Lancaster County, Pennsylvania.

How to Use This Coloring Book

1. Gather supplies: colored pencils, markers, chalk, crayons, or paints and brushes.

2. Pick a coloring page that appeals to you or fits your mood or your life circumstance. Think for a few minutes about colors and patterns you will use. Or page through the book to read the prayers from the Amish prayer book, choosing the prayer that speaks the words of your heart.

3. Test how certain colors would look together by scribbling on a scrap piece of paper before trying it on the drawing. Traditional fraktur colors include deep red or maroon, ochre, orange, blue or indigo, and moss green.

4. Read the Scripture verse and look it up in your Bible to discover the bigger story or context for the verse. The extra reading may inspire you as you color the illustration.

5. Consider whether you will tear out the finished piece to send to someone or frame as a gift for a special friend or loved one.

6. Do not hurry. The idea behind coloring is to relax, meditate, pray, and breathe more slowly. Your coloring page does not have to be perfect!

7. If you sometimes pray through writing, you can also use the blank spaces on the pages to write prayers. You could also journal, perhaps noting when and why you colored a particular fraktur design. Just be sure not to use a pen or marker that will show through to the other side of the page.

8. Thank God for the wisdom of timeless prayers that have survived the centuries and bask in God's love as you color.

_____
_____
_____
_____
_____
_____
_____
_____
_____
_____
_____

Just as you have given us the day for work, so also have you, through your divine kindness, ordained the night for rest. This rest we have enjoyed, merciful God and Father, under your gracious fatherly shelter and keeping. For this it is fitting that we praise, honor, and glorify you from the bottom of our hearts and the depths of our souls.

O heavenly Father, you have again let this day dawn. Help us remember that it is your gracious gift. Teach us to understand gratefully why you are again bestowing this glorious gift. As a merciful Father, you let your beautiful sun rise above our heads.

The day is yours, and yours also the night; you established
the sun and moon.

—Psalm 74:16

6

Teach us to understand.

_____
_____
_____
_____
_____
_____
_____
_____
_____
_____
_____

*H*oly Father, let our bodies rest peacefully, without stain of body or soul, according to your holy and divine will. Likewise, let our hearts, our spirits, and our thoughts remain awake in you forever, looking forward to the coming of your dear Son. May we prepare ourselves in conformity with your divine counsel and await your glorious coming with joy.

Holy and merciful Father, we pray that the light of your divine grace may shine upon us. May we not be overcome by the night of darkness in which the whole world lies, nor fall asleep unto death. Instead, may we pass through death into life. Let this all be to the praise, honor, and glory of your holy, excellent, and majestic name, and to our eternal salvation.

In peace I will lie down and sleep, for you alone, LORD,
make me dwell in safety.

—Psalm 4:8

et our hearts

remain awake in you.

_____

_____

_____

_____

_____

_____

_____

_____

_____

_____

_____

_____

_____

_____

_____

_____

May you, holy Father, always be our path and guide, our refuge and haven, our comfort and strength. Cause your holy and divine Word, which you allow us to hear, to be living and active in our hearts so we may please you and serve you till the end of our life.

Grant us obedient hearts, full of faith, wisdom, and understanding so we will know how we are to live, walk, and please you. Fill our hearts as well with love, peace, and true unity. For your love is the true bond, with which you hold your chosen ones together under your care and protection and through your divine grace and invincible strength.

Your word is a lamp for my feet, a light on my path.

—Psalm 119:105

_____

_____

_____

_____

_____

_____

_____

_____

_____

_____

_____

_____

*W*e praise and thank you, heavenly Father, for creating all things, heaven and earth, the sea and everything in it, and for keeping faith forever. We thank you for bringing justice to the one who suffers injustice, and for all whom you have saved, who have believed and placed their trust in you from the beginning of the world and who have remained in your fear. May you indeed continue to save them.

Give us also a steadfast, living faith and a firm trust, a holy hope, and a genuine love. May we in this manner serve you and keep your commandments wholeheartedly, with joyful souls and with all our strength, to the end, whether unto life or unto death.

Righteousness and justice are the foundation of your
throne; love and faithfulness go before you.

—Psalm 89:14

_____

_____

_____

_____

_____

_____

_____

_____

_____

_____

_____

_____

O holy Father in heaven, feed me with the living heavenly bread of
your holy Word. Give me to drink the living water of your Holy Spirit.
Look upon me always with your holy eyes, that I may turn away from
evil. Protect me also from warfare and bloodshed, from the terrible war
in the land, and from every form of confusion, which might deceive
me and separate me from your love and righteousness. O holy Father
in heaven, do not let the petitions of your dear Child, Jesus Christ, be
lost, nor the prayers of all believers made on my behalf.

> *Whoever drinks the water I give them will never*
> *thirst. Indeed, the water I give them will become in them*
> *a spring of water welling up to eternal life.*

> —John 4:14

_____

_____

_____

_____

_____

_____

_____

_____

_____

_____

_____

_____

*W*e also pray from our hearts for all people who belong to you, for all the concerns of your people for which we can still pray, and for those who heartily desire your grace and our petition. Give all of us your merciful, ever-helping hand and grace, comfort, hope, faith, and love. Strengthen all of us together in the genuine, true faith, in hope and patience, and in true Christian love, faithfulness, and unity. Graciously unite us together in your noble, dear peace, O Father in heaven, rich in love, for the sake of Jesus Christ; help us to love you from our hearts, hanging on to you above all else.

Make my joy complete by being like-minded, having the same love, being one in spirit and of one mind.

—Philippians 2:2

_____

_____

_____

_____

_____

_____

_____

_____

_____

_____

*H*elp us also that we do not depart from your holy Word, either to the right or to the left. Continue to prepare for us a path and a way, a place and a home, a peace and a guide, that in all our dealings we may dwell safely among all our enemies. Look mercifully upon our many weaknesses, and lead us together in your name forever, to hear your holy Word in a useful and fruitful way. Continually draw us together in your mercy, under your powerful hand of grace and under your fatherly care and protection. Take us under your divine grace and power, which cannot be overcome.

For the word of God is alive and active. Sharper than
any double-edged sword, it penetrates even to dividing
soul and spirit, joints and marrow; it judges the thoughts
and attitudes of the heart.

—Hebrews 4:12

_____

_____

_____

_____

_____

_____

_____

_____

_____

_____

_____

*W*e ask you, holy Father, to show your grace and mercy to us all throughout the whole wide world. Graciously draw us together with your blessing, care, and protection. Do not let division and disunity come among us. Kindly safeguard us, O holy, dear Father, from every type of false doctrine and false living, from every kind of mistrust and guile, from false faith and every sort of unkindness, and from every false idea and evil opinion. Indeed, safeguard us graciously from all that might damage or hinder our salvation and joy, from all that might divide us, or lead us away from your love and righteousness, or bring us to neglect your holy Word.

> *Because I consider all your precepts right, I hate every*
> *wrong path. Your statutes are wonderful;*
> *therefore I obey them.*
>
> —Psalm 119:128-129

Through the thanksgiving of many devout people, may your holy name be honored and glorified. O Lord, rich in love, true God in heaven, create forever a sure path and entrance for your holy Word. Let it grow and multiply, and may it also be planted elsewhere as far as this is possible, that we all may be taught and instructed correctly. Feed and give drink to all who hunger and thirst after your kingdom and after your love and righteousness, according to your holy Word and gospel. We also pray, O holy Father, for all faithful messengers, servants, and ministers whom you have sent out to proclaim and preach your holy Word and righteousness.

Blessed are those who hunger and thirst for righteousness,
for they will be filled.

—Matthew 5:6

Feed all who hunger

_____

_____

_____

_____

_____

_____

_____

_____

_____

_____

*G*ive us as well a true, steadfast, and living faith, a genuine Christian love and uprightness, a good and blessed hope in you, O Lord, and also a steadfast trust in your goodness and great mercy. Also help us that from our whole heart and soul we may keep this trust with you and with your holy Word. May we indeed love you from our hearts with all our strength, holding to you and serving you truly until our final end, both in living and in dying.

Help us that we may be able to serve you truly and have a heartfelt desire to hold to your commandments as long as we live, as much as is possible through your grace.

Jesus replied: "'Love the Lord your God with all your heart and with all your soul and with all your mind.'"

—Matthew 22:37

_____

_____

_____

_____

_____

_____

_____

_____

_____

_____

We thank you humbly and from our hearts and declare to you our deep praise, honor, and glory and our highest thanksgiving, O Lord God, rich in love! We thank you for all your great deeds of kindness and fatherly faithfulness, and for your great gifts and acts of mercy that you have always shown to us and done for us, and especially now in these last, dark times. You keep faith forever and create justice for those who often need to suffer much injustice. But you have also redeemed all those who have held to you throughout all time, who have believed, trusted, and served you truly and have feared you constantly.

I live in a high and holy place, but also with the one who
is contrite and lowly in spirit, to revive the spirit of the
lowly and to revive the heart of the contrite.

—Isaiah 57:15

_____
_____
_____
_____
_____
_____
_____
_____
_____
_____

O highly praised Son of God! O faithful Savior of all those chosen throughout the world! O Lord, rich in love, we thank you with deep humility. From our hearts we thank you for all your suffering and death, your merit and atonement, for all your unspeakable agony and torment, sufferings and the shedding of your innocent blood, even unto death.

You have borne all this, and for us willingly and with great patience you suffered death, through which you intend to redeem and save us from eternal disgrace and torment. For this, may you be highly praised into all eternity, O patient slaughtered Lamb!

Worthy is the Lamb, who was slain, to receive power and
wealth and wisdom and strength and honor and glory
and praise!

—Revelation 5:12

_____
_____
_____
_____
_____
_____
_____
_____
_____
_____
_____
_____

So we ask now, O Father, clothe us with the genuine, true faith, with your true love, faithfulness, and truth, and with the power of your Holy Spirit. Above all things, may we honor, fear, and love you, O Father, with our whole heart, with the desire of our souls, with willing hearts and minds, and may we keep your commandments until the end of our lives. This we ask in the name of our Lord Jesus Christ.

We also pray, O holy Father, that you might show us the petition of your dear Child, Jesus Christ, and protect us from all evil, and keep us in your truth and in your holy name.

May your priests be clothed with your righteousness; may your faithful people sing for joy.

—Psalm 132:9

_____

_____

_____

_____

_____

_____

_____

_____

_____

_____

_____

_____

*W*e faithfully pray, O holy Father, place in our hearts wisdom and reason from above, that we may properly acknowledge our sins and then avoid them. May we thus mend our ways and repent.

We pray, O holy Father, strengthen our faith, increase our love, and align our hearts with the true and pure love of God and the patience of Jesus Christ. May we live and walk at all times in the path of peace and your divine love. May we not desire anything more than you, O Lord, and your holy and divine Word, your law, and your righteousness.

For the LORD gives wisdom; from his mouth come
knowledge and understanding.

—Proverbs 2:6

Direct our hearts in the way of peace so we may have peace with all people, as far as it is possible for us. May we love our enemies, bless those who curse us, and do good in return for the evil inflicted upon us. Also help us gladly to share our homes and lodging with others, feed the hungry, give drink to those who thirst, shelter guests, clothe the naked, and visit the sick and imprisoned, as much as you demand of us. We faithfully pray, O holy Father, also grant us grace, that we always may strive for peace, for salvation and love, without which no one shall see the Lord.

But I tell you, love your enemies and pray for those who persecute you.

—Matthew 5:44

We faithfully pray, O holy Father, grant us growth and maturity, and make your Word living and strong in our hearts. Thus may your holy Word also bear fruit in our hearts, unto the praise and glory of your most holy name, as well as for the needs and consolation of our poor souls.

We also utter truly our highest praise and thanksgiving to you for good health, which you have provided and given us, and also for our good place in this land, for house and shelter. We thank you for all your holy and worthy gifts and acts of grace that you have shown and provided for us each day and hour. May you be praised now and from everlasting to everlasting.

I have hidden your word in my heart that I might not
sin against you.

—Psalm 119:11

_____
_____
_____
_____
_____
_____
_____
_____
_____
_____
_____

O faithful God, sole refuge of the forsaken, listen to us in accord with your wonderful righteousness. God, our salvation, you are the refuge for everyone upon the earth, as well as far away on the sea. You are our shelter forever and ever. Even before the mountains existed, before the earth and the world were created, you are, O God, from everlasting to everlasting. Be with us wherever we are, accompany us, and care for us. For the earth is the Lord's and the fullness thereof; the world, and all that dwells therein.

Lord, your grace extends as far as the heavens and your truth as far as the clouds.

Lord, you have been our dwelling place throughout all generations. Before the mountains were born or you brought forth the whole world, from everlasting to everlasting you are God.

—Psalm 90:1-2

Blessed is the one whose help comes from the God of Jacob, whose hope rests in the Lord God, who created heaven, earth, the sea, and everything in it, who keeps faith forever, who metes out justice for those who suffer violence and injustice, who feeds the hungry. The Lord redeems the imprisoned, the Lord opens the eyes of the blind. The Lord raises up those who have been struck down. The Lord loves the righteous. The Lord protects the strangers and orphans, keeps the widows, and turns back the way of the ungodly. The Lord is king forever, your God, O Zion, for all generations. Hallelujah! Amen.

For all those who exalt themselves will be humbled, and
those who humble themselves will be exalted.

—Luke 14:11

_____
_____
_____
_____
_____
_____
_____
_____
_____
_____

Come, King of mercies! Fill me here in this life with your mercy so that you may fill me with your eternal glory. In this, your kingdom of grace, rule over me with your Holy Spirit. Indeed, establish in me your kingdom, which is righteousness, peace, and joy in the Holy Spirit.

Illuminate my heart, purify my life, sanctify my thoughts, that they may be reverent and pleasing to you. Enfold me in your grace, that I may never fall away.

Come to us, Holy Trinity! Renovate us as your dwelling and temple, and kindle in us the light of your knowledge, faith, love, hope, humility, patience, prayer, perseverance, and fear of God.

Blessed are the merciful, for they will be shown mercy.

—Matthew 5:7

Remain with us, Lord Jesus Christ, according to your promise, every day until the end of the world. Do not forsake your children and your church as orphans; otherwise they have no father on earth.

Lord, our Ruler, spread your glorious name throughout the earth so that there is thanksgiving to you in heaven. May you, in accord with the praise celebrated through the mouths of babes and infants, pass judgment so that you may destroy the enemy and the avenger.

You, O Lord Christ, are the fairest among those who inhabit the earth. Most gracious are your lips, for which God has blessed you eternally.

Remain in me, as I also remain in you. No branch can bear fruit by itself; it must remain in the vine. Neither can you bear fruit unless you remain in me.

—John 15:4

_____

_____

_____

_____

_____

_____

_____

_____

_____

_____

_____

*A*nd since you are also the King of glory, make us citizens in your kingdom of glory. When you come in your great power and glory, and all the holy angels with you, you will be sitting on the throne of your glory. Fill us then with those words of joy. Father, I desire that those also, whom you have given to me, may be with me where I am so that they may see your glory. Come here, you who have been blessed by my Father, inherit the kingdom that has been prepared for you from the beginning! Amen.

For the joy set before him he endured the cross, scorning
its shame, and sat down at the right hand of the
throne of God.

—Hebrews 12:2

_____
_____
_____
_____
_____
_____
_____
_____
_____
_____

*M*ay this blessing also come upon me. Grant that my family and I may eat from your kind fatherly hand, as do the birds of the sky, who neither sow nor reap. Yet you, heavenly Father, feed them. Each year you clothe the lilies and flowers of the field with new robes. Indeed, each year you grant every creature a new body after its kind. You also will certainly not forget me and my family, for you, heavenly Father, know what all we need. Hence, teach me above everything else to seek your kingdom and your righteousness so that, in line with your promise, you will fulfill my temporal needs as well.

*Consider how the wild flowers grow. They do not labor
or spin. Yet I tell you, not even Solomon in all his
splendor was dressed like one of these.*

—Luke 12:27

_____
_____
_____
_____
_____
_____
_____
_____
_____
_____
_____

*T*his, however, is my consolation: you have said, You shall befriend the
orphans and widows and strangers, and give them food and clothing,
and stand in fear of the Lord your God. So this also is my comfort: it
is written, The Lord raises the thirsty from the dust and lifts high the
poor from the filth, placing them among the princes, and letting them
inherit the throne of honor. You, dear Father, have thus ordained that
the rich and the poor must dwell together. Yet you, Lord, have made
them all. You yourself say, It is better to be poor and walk devoutly
than to be rich and walk in perverse ways.

He has brought down rulers from their thrones but has
lifted up the humble. He has filled the hungry with good
things but has sent the rich away empty.

—Luke 1:52-53

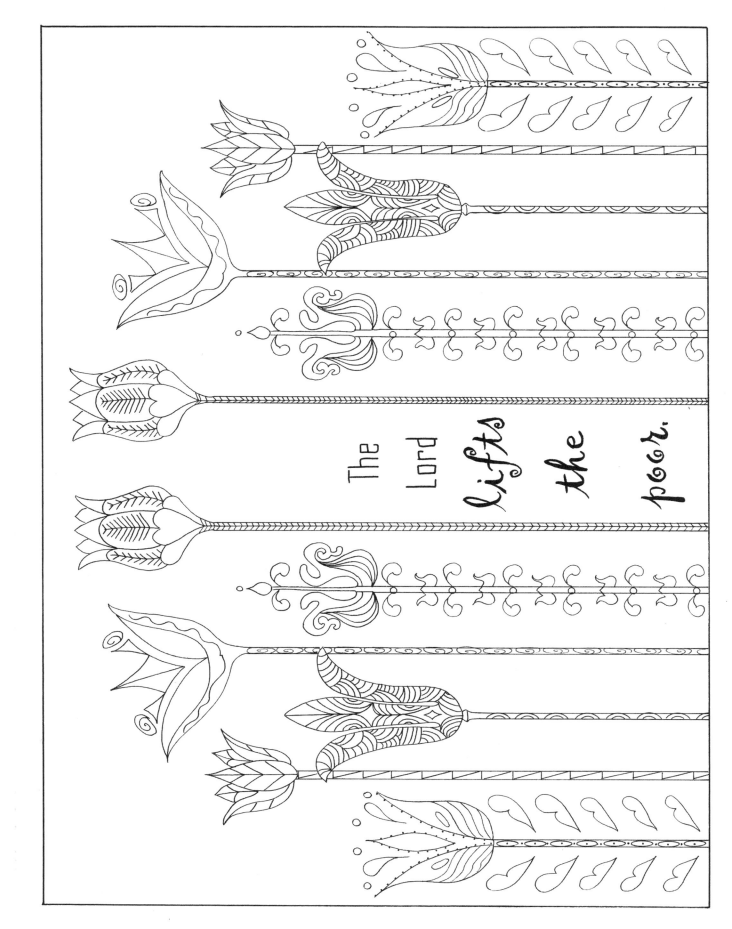

The Lord lifts the poor.

_____

_____

_____

_____

_____

_____

_____

_____

_____

_____

*T*he Lord cares for me. I hope that I may also see the goodness of the Lord in the land of the living. Be comforted and courageous, you who wait confidently for the Lord. God, you have created me to praise you. Grant that I may love you worthily. You are the most majestic, the one most worthy of praise, the most holy, the most righteous, the most beautiful, the most gracious, the most friendly; indeed, you are the one most true. You are just in all your works, holy in all your ways. You are the most wise. All your works from eternity are known to you. You are the most powerful; none can oppose you.

I remain confident of this: I will see the goodness of
the LORD in the land of the living. Wait for the LORD;
be strong and take heart and wait for the LORD.

—Psalm 27:13-14

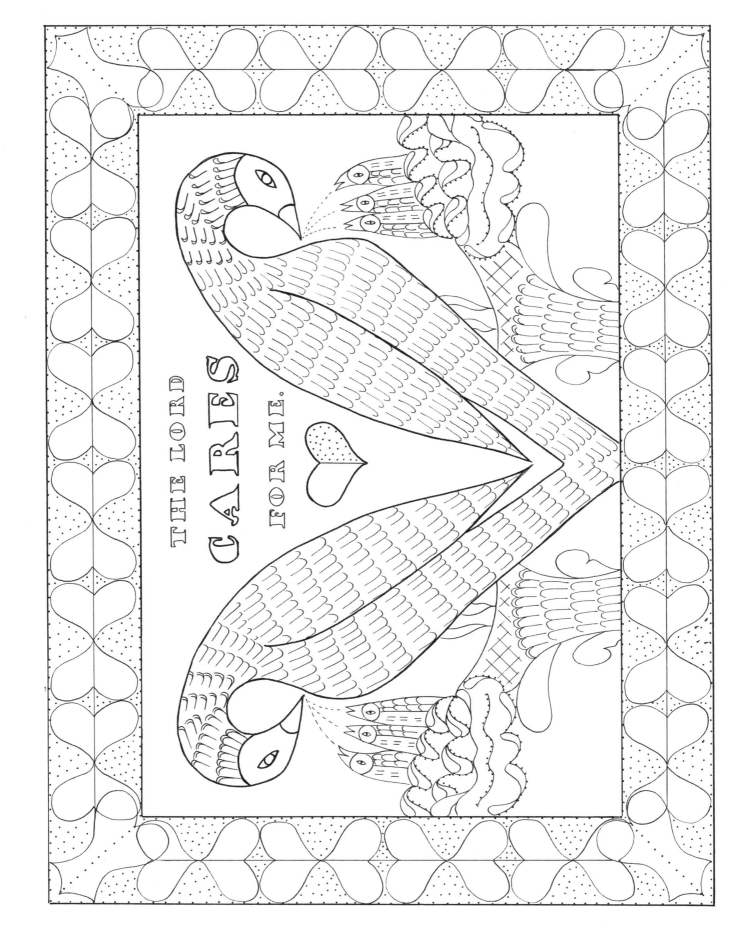

_____

_____

_____

_____

_____

_____

_____

_____

_____

_____

Y ou are also very gracious, merciful, patient, of great good, and you soon regret the punishment you apply. You do not remain angry forever, and you do not remember sins forever. As great as your omnipotence is, just as great is your mercy. Your strength is endless, and your compassion is eternal.

O eternal Light, O eternal Salvation, O eternal Love, O eternal Sweetness! Let me see you, let me experience you, let me taste you.

In you I find everything I lack in this life of misery. You are full and overflowing, and outside of you is vain poverty, wretchedness, and misery. Life without you is bitter death. Your goodness is better than life.

The LORD, the LORD, the compassionate and gracious
God, slow to anger, abounding in love and faithfulness.

—Exodus 34:6

Almighty, merciful God! You so graciously permit the light of your grace to shine upon many hearts, just as it enlightens dark places. Help us that we may truly become children of peace through your peaceable, eternal gospel. Give grace and power to those with hands raised [in prayer], give strength to the weak, and give steadfastness to the strong, that they may all follow your Word.

Thus, we humbly pray, think of your previous mercy, of your great acts of goodness with which you often saved the Israelites from their enemies. Think of your mighty strength and power with which you continue to save the true Israel according to the Spirit—all those chosen Christian believers—from every error, oppression, fear, and need.

Peace I leave with you; my peace I give you. I do not
give to you as the world gives. Do not let your hearts be
troubled and do not be afraid.

—John 14:27

_____
_____
_____
_____
_____
_____
_____
_____
_____
_____

O Lord God, omnipotent, heavenly, gracious Father! Give us poor, needy, impoverished people the spirit of wisdom and the revelation of your knowledge. Enlighten the eyes of our understanding. Strengthen us all in faith, and let that faith grow in Jesus Christ. Grant us a resolute hope in your mercy, in contrast to the shortsightedness of our sinful conscience. Grant us a well-founded, well-fashioned love for you and for all people, for your sake. We pray that you would strengthen our poor and weak consciences. Endow us with the living, actual strength of your equally omnipotent Word in the Holy Spirit.

The LORD is my strength and my defense; he has become
my salvation. He is my God, and I will praise him, my
father's God, and I will exalt him.

—Exodus 15:2

72

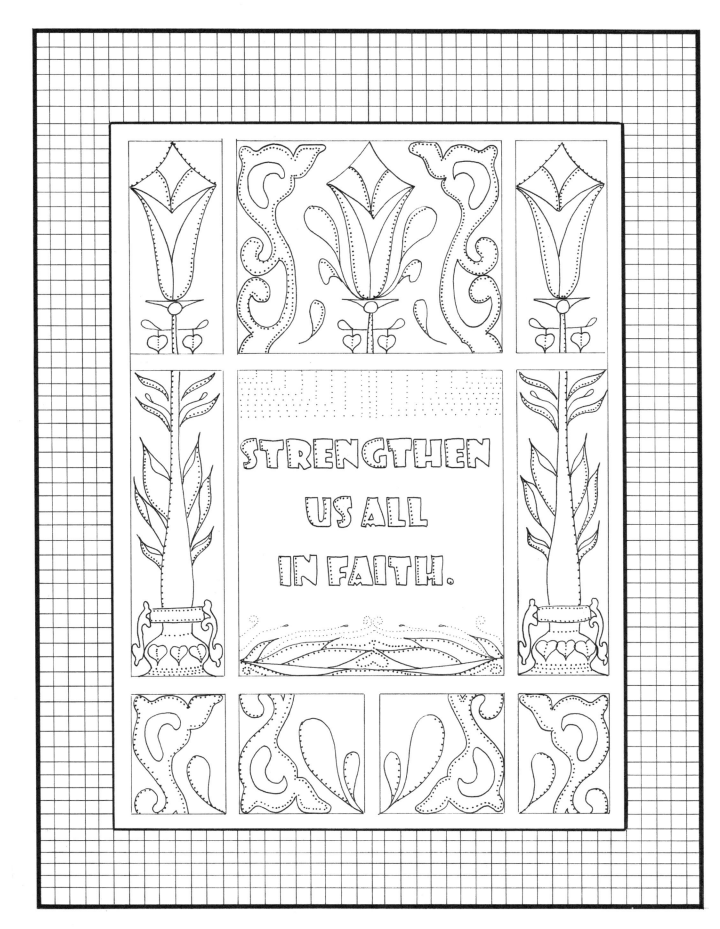

Eternal, merciful God, you are a God of peace, love, and unity, not of conflict and division. With this unity you view the world in your righteous judgment, knowing it has forsaken you. You alone can establish and maintain unity in a world that in its own wisdom has fallen away from you, especially in those things that relate to your divine truth and the salvation of souls. You let the world divide and splinter into pieces so that with the false wisdom of disunity, which can only lead to disgrace, the world might again turn to you, O Lover of unity!

Make every effort to keep the unity of the Spirit through
the bond of peace.

—Ephesians 4:3

_O_ most beloved Comforter of disconsolate hearts. O worthy Guest of believing souls. O sweet Refreshment and only Sustainer in our weakness! Do not depart from us. Along with God the Father and the Son, make an eternal dwelling in us. Strengthen our weak eyes. Wash all that is impure in us. Heal all the wounds in our flesh. Make straight what is lame and crooked. Renew whatever has grown cold in producing goodness. Lead and guide onto the right path whatever has gone astray and become lost.

O most holy Light! Illuminate with the brilliance of your grace the inner recesses of the hearts of your faithful, who today are again submitting themselves to your discipline, teaching, and comfort.

"But I will restore you to health and heal your wounds,"
declares the LORD.

—Jeremiah 30:17

_____

_____

_____

_____

_____

_____

_____

_____

_____

_____

_We_ take comfort in one thing only: that Jesus Christ, the Son of God, took mercy upon us. For this we declare to him our praise and thanks, with heartfelt hope, that he may never forsake us. We also believe that in the presence of his heavenly Father, he without ceasing is representing us and indeed all who have submitted to him.

Since you, O Holy Spirit, are the Spirit of the Lord Christ, permit us to enjoy such faithfulness, love, and graciousness. Pour your mighty strength into us. Grant a new, reborn heart to those of us who are weak in faith yet who now are submitting to your discipline in word and heart.

He gives strength to the weary and increases the power
of the weak.

—Isaiah 40:29

Have mercy on me, O Jesus, Son of David! If you so desire, you can certainly help me.

O look upon me graciously, I pray from the depths of my heart, and save me from my temptation. O Father, pour out your mercy upon me and comfort me again with your fatherly help. With David, I call to you from my heart, O dear God and Father! Create in me a pure heart, O God, and give me a new and right Spirit, that henceforth I may serve you in love, in trust, in safety, and in childlike hope, humbly and with my whole heart.

Have mercy on me, O God, according to your unfailing love; according to your great compassion blot out my transgressions.

—Psalm 51:1

_____
_____
_____
_____
_____
_____
_____
_____
_____
_____

*W*e poor children do not live by bread alone, but by every word that proceeds from your mouth, according to the testimony of your beloved Son, Jesus Christ. In his name we now are assembled here in your presence to proclaim, to hear, and to understand what is your holy and divine will for us. You, O God, have kindled in us this zeal and have put into our hearts this desire and love for this work. Thus we have gladly and freely gathered for that purpose, coming together in a spirit of unity. We thank and praise you for all of this from the depth of our hearts.

With praise and thanksgiving they sang to the LORD:
"He is good; his love toward Israel endures forever." And
all the people gave a great shout of praise to the LORD.

—Ezra 3:11

_____
_____
_____
_____
_____
_____
_____
_____
_____
_____
_____

O Lord, seal this truth in our hearts. Yes, dear Father, strengthen our confidence to enable us to fathom how deeply you love the human race, to which you are so inclined and willing to give every good gift. May we firmly trust your almighty power, for we know that you, O God, make no promises that you cannot abundantly fulfill. Since you desire our well-being even more than we ourselves do, grant us not to look upon our unworthiness, but only upon your kindness, goodness, truth, and unlimited power.

May we ask or desire only what is pleasing to you, O God, to your praise and for the salvation of our souls.

How priceless is your unfailing love, O God! People take
refuge in the shadow of your wings.

—Psalm 36:7

_____
_____
_____
_____
_____
_____
_____
_____
_____
_____

You alone are wise. Not only do you live in the light, but you yourself are the eternal light. We are living here in this dark, blind world; so enlighten us, O God, with your divine wisdom, which is a coworker of your throne. Send down your wisdom from your holy heaven and the throne of your glory to be with us and work with us so we may know what is pleasing to you. Without this gift, O God, we cannot please you. For this wisdom, Lord, we also ask in the name of your beloved Son, Jesus Christ, in whom is hidden all the riches of wisdom and knowledge.

The people walking in darkness have seen a great light;
on those living in the land of deep darkness a light
has dawned.

—Isaiah 9:2

Lord, almighty God, dear heavenly Father, you have led your people through the ministry of the only great Shepherd of your sheep, Jesus Christ, through the blood of the eternal covenant, which he shed for us on the cross for our reconciliation. For this we give you praise and thanks, blessing and honor and everlasting glory, through your Son, the same Jesus Christ, our Lord. Since you are the Provider of all, you open your kind hand and pour out your goodness and blessing upon those whose hope is in you, whose eyes look up to you. So help us, Lord, to turn the eyes of our hearts to you in trust.

Who then is the one who condemns? No one. Christ Jesus who died—more than that, who was raised to life—is at the right hand of God and is also interceding for us.

—Romans 8:34